<u>Hanukah:</u>
A Story Of Lights

To Enter The Palace Of Wisdom

Child-Time Publishers

Established 1988

www.childtimepublishers.com

Library of Congress Number: 2018900818

First Edition: January 2018

ISBN: 978-0-929934-11-2 (softcover)

Cover Art/Painting: Arlene Kingston

Logo Design: Sabina K. Mintz & Eric Sander Kingston

Photos Of Eric Sander Kingston By: William Kingston

Printed In USA

W.o.W.

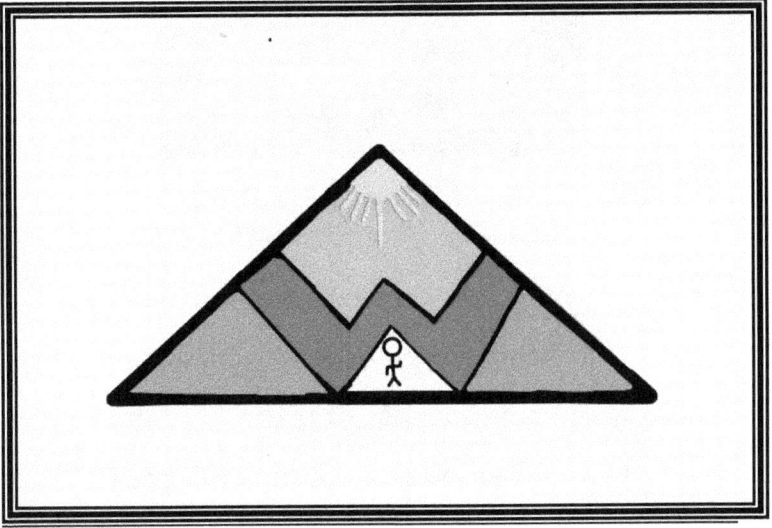

Wish On Wisdom ™

There was once a person, who was granted from Heaven, a wish. They could either wish for wealth, or wish for wisdom. The person replied: "I wish for wisdom. For through wisdom, I will attain great wealth."

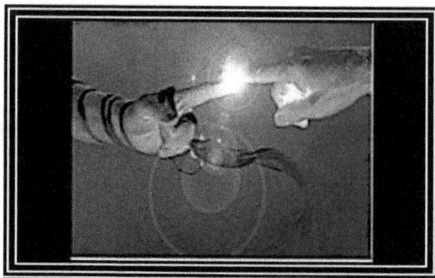

How To Use This Book

10 Power Prayer Of Divine Protection

1. May you surpass your teachers

2. May you go beyond yourself

3. May you leave a legacy of truth, love and justice

4. May you be an example of dignity

5. May your powers be used to unite all people, "not serve the vanity" of a single person

6. May you always be grateful for the smallest of things

7. May you never say "yes" when you mean "no"

8. May all your past hurts become the lessons that guide you towards your constructive destiny

9. May you see the greatest strength is within, when it connects constructively to others

And most of all

10. May you see, "The pain you feel is from the love you withhold."

Hanukah:

A Story Of Lights

What proves G-d's Love & the Love of G-d's Will
Those eight days of Light, they're burning still!

Table Of Contents

Hanukah: A Story Of Lights

Hanukah is a celebration of joy and of tears
Of how a people survived and would not disappear
It's a story of G-d, and honor and might
And the sacred oil that burned for eight Holy Nights

Hanukah's a dedication and a festival remembering a time
That the Light of our ages continues to shine
It's a triumph of freedom, whose example says clear…
"G-d's Light defeats darkness with His brave hero's tears"

Now, this story's of bravery, of conquest, of faith
To a people put to the test, who would not run or break
So, I pass on this telling, from me now to you
The story of the Maccabee's, some of G-d's bravest Jews!

Now, these Jews would not bow, or bend, or shake
Or kneel to false gods that neither help or create
And despite all the punishment these Jews would endure
Faith was their honor for their G-d sustained the world

And the women among them, where just as brave
To give what was most precious, to set examples and save
There's the story of Hannah and her seven sons
Who each lost their lives, rather then bend before one…

7

Who called himself king Antiochus, the ruler of world's
Yet, all he showed was a tyranny hurled
So, each son was brought before him and told to bow low
Before graven images that contained no Holy Glow

But none would do so, no matter the price
Proving their devotion to G-d saying, "My faith is my life!"
And as Hannah's last son fell with a cry
The Blessed Holy One heard our peoples cry

King Antiochus fell on the temples, pushing over steeples
And tried to force and destroy G-d's Chosen People
He tore mother from child and split husband and wife
And painted the sun like the darkest midnight

Then, this false king and his sinful people
Tried to force their beliefs on the souls and G-d's People
He ordered mothers and children, now to be sold
And the king put into slavery that which he did not own

Now, all seemed dark and there seemed no way
And night came down and held onto the day
But suddenly Heaven opened up wide
The L-rd put a Hammer into some souls and some minds

In the village of Modi'in, the Hasmonean family lived
Where Mattathias Maccabee did honor and give
He saw an officer of the king come and approach
The Things they did honor and cherish the most

Mattathias made a decision that had to be made
They would not go on broken, beaten or enslaved!
So, he struck out a blow and cried out his creed
"All those who are for the L-rd, follow me!"

Then, Mattathias gathered his sons and they began
To fight with the honor and for liberty's plans
Then men without training added strength to the cause
Understanding,
Their faith must survive as One in G-d's Law

And the L-rd helped their struggles, a bit more each day
The faith was strong, but strength swaggered and swayed
And they prayed,
"Who is like You, Adonai, among other G-d's?"
None!!!
For we are Your Children, Your Hammer, Your Rod!"

Then, the battle before them they could not lose
For the freewill of a people must have freedom to choose
Then, an Angel saw the battle and knew what to do
So, The Blessed Holy One gave them ALL
The strength of ten men - *plus two!!!*

They attacked from the hills and fought through the night
For this was a battle of the dark and the light
And G-d delivered the many to the hands of the few
And the impure fell from these pious war Jews

Then, the good woman Judith struck an evil general down
And the enemies fled saying,
"If the Jewish woman are this strong,
Let us not face the men in this town!"
And the finale battle came and G-d stood by their side
Then, the evil armies fled away and our freedom survived

And the Jew's returned and cleaned out the grounds
And a once sacred container of oil was found
And it burned and it burned with its sacred light
Eight days it shone to represent Jewish Light

Then, all gathered 'round the Temple to thank and pray
And offer their love for the Blessed Holy Ones Ways
For in their rededication of the Temple they did seed
Saying,
"This prayer of love and thanks, to G-d for sustaining
The Lights and great Deeds:"

They said...

Dear G-d,
Who rules all the worlds,
Who gave us the Torah, a most sacred of pearls
We give unto you our prayers and our lights
To the One who gave unto us the great spark of life

We put you before all other things
Your Great Name we honor, Your Sabbath we keep
We fight if we have to, to preserve Your Blessed Way

But none of us can stand before Your most Holy of Names

Yet, deep in our hearts, on the tears of our souls
We can't know all Your great Ways, but this much we know
We are your people, no matter the cause
We must stand with what was given - Sinai's Great Law

We must love one another, for the future must fill
The seeds of Your Commandments that shine from the hill
You sustain all the righteous with Your most Holy Glow
And to tomorrow's children, this they must know

We of the past, say unto you
That the Glory of G-d is the light within you
So, gaze at the candles and remember your past
It's calling for you to remember and forever last

It's a light that shines brightly from G-d's most Holy Will
That says,
The candles of yesterday are calling you still!!!

So remember,
Your's is a people who would not disappear
No matter the odds, no matter the years
So many people have come and have gone
But yours is the people who says, "Carry on strong!"
Shema Yisrael, we are one, we belong
So, we of your past say, "Carry on, carry on"
We of your past say, "Carry on, carry on"

These life lessons are not easy to learn
They're not easy to teach or for love to discern
Yet, just as one candle, lights all the others
-the Maccabee's remind us, through G-d-
How we still need one another

So, we must rage against the darkness of night
Remembering the soul of man reflects G-d's Sacred Light
For yours is a people stronger than chain or hate's flames
Because what hate destroys,
Will rise,
Rebuilt through G-d's Love again

Yes, this was a retelling of our hero's brave cries
Where we stood against tyranny to help freedom survive
For the message of Hanukah goes beyond race or creed
It's a story of a people whose light was G-d's Need

Now we must remember this most sacred of tales
Of how G-d gives us our hammer
When our own strength fails
For what proves G-d's Love and the Love of G-d's Will
Those eight days of Light, they're burning still!

So, light each of your candles and remember your past
The songs and the dreidel and the tears and the dance
The Menorah and the Temple that still holds Its stand
For the Eternal Light of your people shall never end

As the Tribes and the Temple shall rise and amend
As the faith of your people shall never bend
As the soul of our Torah always defends
As the Lights of G-d Glory will forever transcend

ACKNOWLEDGEMENTS

I would like to thank my mother & father, William & Arlene Kingston, as well as my sister, Wendy & her husband Eric S. Mintz & my nieces Sabina & Juliet.

The Love Between You

Written For

My Father & Mother,

William & Arlene Kingston

The Love Between You

One day,
Two soul-mates who had spent a whole lifetime together
Were going over the events of their lives.
As they looked over their many struggles and hardships,
They noticed that during their worst moments
It seemed that it was only each other
That pulled the other through,
It seemed that it was only their togetherness and faith
That held their lives together.

One day the L-rd appeared before them and they asked,
"L-rd, during our worst trials and tribulations
It seems it was only our togetherness
That held our lives together,
It seemed was only our togetherness
That kept our faith alive,
Where in all this was the Presence of G-d?"

The L-rd replied: "My precious children,
My beautiful Creations
I
Was the love between you"

ABOUT ERIC

Eric Sander Kingston is a master strategist, martial artist and composer. Best known for rapid transformational techniques, Eric uses a specifically created system of strategic drills, martial arts, original writings, to transfer specific techniques, and practical tools, to his clients. Eric's system empowers people to breakthrough their fear, and cultivate a deep, internal power of awareness, allowing them greater access to achieve their goals, and cultivate a life of stability and sustainable success.

Connect with Eric directly, for personal, or group, training, consultation, custom written works, or to have Eric personally transform your corporation or event, visit:

www.ericsanderkingston.com

Wish On Wisdom Philosophy

Every race, religion and region has great wisdom to offer humanity. The Wish On Wisdom parables seek to impart this wisdom to create bridges of unity between all peoples of our planet earth.

www.wishonwisdom.com

"Our most basic common link is that we all inhabit this same small planet. We all breathe the same air. We all cherish our children's future. And we are all mortal."

John F. Kennedy

OTHER PUBLICATIONS
BY CHILD-TIME PUBLISHERS:

Established 1988

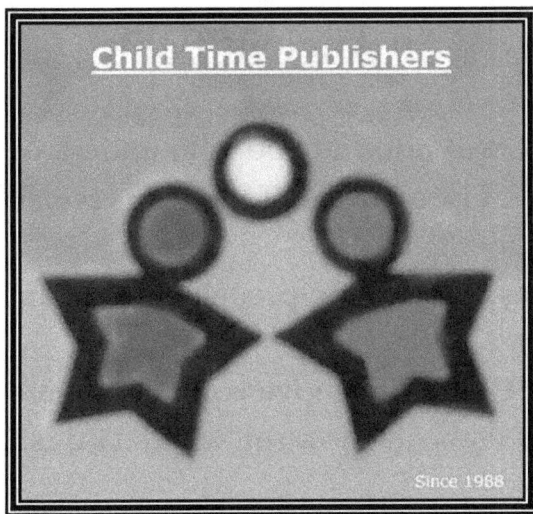

www.childtimepublishers.com

THERE IS NO PLACE WHERE G-D IS NOT

The Wisdom Of A Child Teacher

An Ancient Fable

There was once a child who understood all
The answers of the Universe.

One day, a person approached them and said:

"Child, I will give you one orange
If you can show me where G-d is."

The child replied:

"And I will give you two oranges
If you can show me where G-d is not!"

The story of Mr. Knott's and the Child teacher who enlightens him.

There Is No Place
Where G-d Is Not

The Wisdom Of A Child Teacher

Eric Sander Kingston

AFRICAN WOMEN'S WISDOM
Original Parables
Based On The Proverbs Of Africa
To Empower The Feminine
Written By Eric Sander Kingston

Original one paragraph Parables with an interactive edge designed for personal power and transformation based upon the wisdom of African culture.

African Women's Wisdom

ORIGINAL PARABLES
BASED ON THE PROVERBS OF
AFRICA

By Eric Sander Kingston

THE SACRED GATES

VOLUME 1

13 Original Rabbinic Parables
To Enter The Palace Of Wisdom

The 13 Original Rabbinic Parables within this book are meant to be flexible, practical and interactive. The parables teach universal wisdom's applicable, through the readers interpretation, to any race, religion or region. Each parable concludes with an Insight, Question and Agreement, one can choose to use for further spiritual development.

The Sacred Gates

13 ORIGINAL PARABLES TO ENTER
THE PALACE OF WISDOM

Eric Sander Kingston

The Christmas Heart
Of Childhood

The story of the Christmas Heart & The Prince of
Christmas Town who guards the youth of the world
Written In Rhyme Form.

This is my story
With a bright Christmas glow

Remember,

The dreams of your youth
Are lighter than snow

The Christmas Heart Of Childhood

And The Prince Who Guards It

Eric Sander Kingston

THE PRIMORDIAL WAY
Strategies To Inner Self Mastery
Written By Eric Sander Kingston

Eric Sander Kingston's newest book on internal strategy & philosophy of inner conflict to achieve non-duality and start transforming inner fears.

Please Note: This book is NOT intended for beginners who do not have some background in ancient energy literature, conflict resolution based on transformation towards inner mutual understanding or for Martial Artists who do not grasp Gandhi's Wisdom: *"The greatest demons in the world are those running around our own hearts."*

"It does not matter how many men you defeat! If you do not conquer your inner demons, you will pass your demons onto your child as your parent passed theirs onto you."

From the Film Dragon

The Primordial Way

Strategies To Inner Self Mastery

By Master Strategist
Eric Sander Kingston

THE SACRED GATES

VOLUME 2

13 Original Rabbinic Parables
To Enter The Palace Of Wisdom

The 13 Original Rabbinic Parables within this book are meant to be flexible, practical and interactive. The parables teach universal wisdom's applicable, through the readers interpretation, to any race, religion or region. Each parable concludes with an Insight, Question and Agreement, one can choose to use for further spiritual development.

VOLUME 2

The Sacred Gates

13 ORIGINAL PARABLES TO ENTER
THE PALACE OF WISDOM

Eric Sander Kingston

THE HIDDEN DOOR
26 Original Rabbinic Parables
To Reveal The Concealed

This book is created and intended to be interactive. The book contains 26 original, one paragraph, Jewish wisdom-based parables. These parables are carefully written, and designed, to reveal a practical, universal insight and spiritual awareness. Each parable concludes with an I.Q.A. (Insight, Question, Agreement). This is an optional, proactive opportunity, designed to offer to the reader or listener, an access key that can open an internal door to a personal transformation.

The Hidden Door

26 ORIGINAL RABBINIC PARABLES
TO REVEAL THE CONCEALED

Eric Sander Kingston

Co-Author Steve L. Cohn

The Bagels Are Coming!

A Humorous Look At How Bagels Bring Peace To The World.

Written and Illustrated by Arlene Kingston

Paperback,

Library Of Congress Number: 88-63105

ISBN: 0-929934-00-8
ISBN: 0-929934-00-8

A HUMOROUS LOOK AT HOW BAGELS BRING PEACE TO THE WORLD

THE BAGELS ARE COMING!

by arlene Kingston

NOTES

www.ingramcontent.com/pod-product-compliance
Lightning Source LLC
Chambersburg PA
CBHW060636030426
42337CB00018B/3383